GRAPHIC LIBRARY™

GRAPHIC BIOGRAPHIES

MARTIN LUTHER KING JR.

GREAT CIVIL RIGHTS LEADER

by Jennifer Fandel

illustrated by Brian Bascle

Consultant:

Charles P. Henry

Associate Professor of African American Studies

University of California, Berkeley

Capstone press

Mankato, Minnesota

Graphic Library is published by Capstone Press,
151 Good Counsel Drive, P.O. Box 669, Mankato, Minnesota 56002.
www.capstonepub.com

Books published by Capstone Press are manufactured with paper
containing at least 10 percent post-consumer waste.

Library of Congress Cataloging-in-Publication Data
Fandel, Jennifer.
   Martin Luther King, Jr.: great civil rights leader / by Jennifer Fandel; illustrated by
Brian Bascle
   p. cm.—(Graphic library. Graphic biographies)
   Includes bibliographical references and index.
   ISBN-13: 978-0-7368-6498-5 (hardcover)   ISBN-10: 0-7368-6498-9 (hardcover)
   ISBN-13: 978-0-7368-9661-0 (softcover pbk.)   ISBN-10: 0-7368-9661-9 (softcover pbk.)
   1. King, Martin Luther, Jr., 1929–1968—Juvenile literature. 2. African Americans—
Biography—Juvenile literature. 3. Civil rights workers—United States—Biography—Juvenile
literature. 4. Baptists—United States—Clergy—Biography—Juvenile literature. 5. African
Americans—Civil rights—History—20th century—Juvenile literature. 6. Civil rights
movements—United States—History—20th century—Juvenile literature. I. Title. II. Series.
E185.97.K5F36 2007
323.092—dc22   2006014731

Designer
Jason Knudson

Editor
Mandy Robbins

Editor's note: Direct quotations from primary sources are indicated by a yellow background.

Direct quotations appear on the following pages:
Page 7, from Stanford University website. *The Papers of Martin Luther King, Jr.,* http://www.
   stanford.edu/group/King/index.htm.
Pages 20, 21, 23, 25, from *A Call to Conscience: The Landmark Speeches of Dr. Martin Luther
   King, Jr.,* edited by Clayborne Carson and Kris Shepard (New York: IPM/Warner
   Books, 2001).

Printed in the United States of America in Stevens Point, Wisconsin.
052012
006738

TABLE OF CONTENTS

CHAPTER 1

A BLACK AND WHITE WORLD

Martin Luther King Jr., was born in Atlanta, Georgia, in 1929. At age 6, Martin was playing with a friend. That day was the last time the two boys would play together.

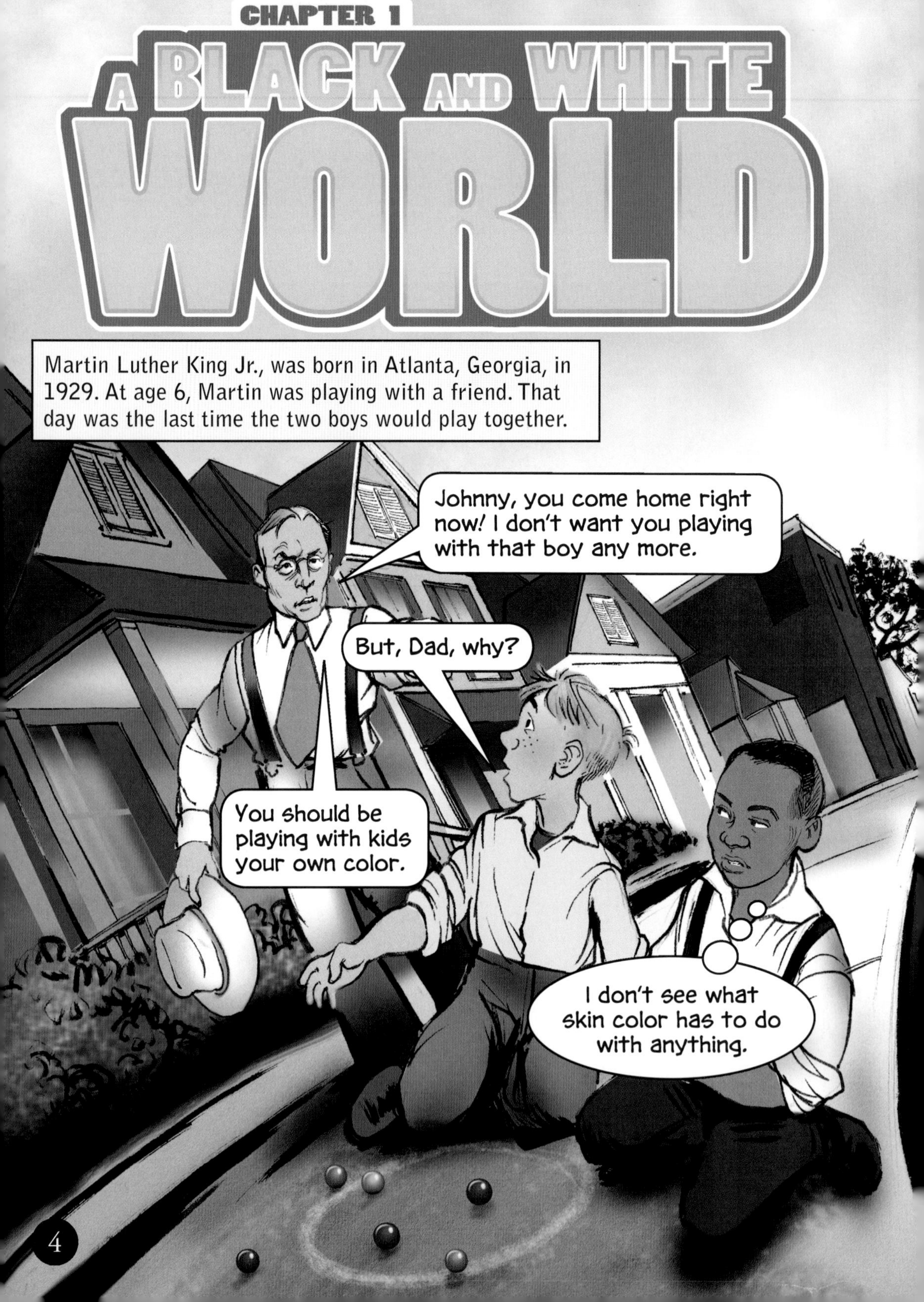
Johnny, you come home right now! I don't want you playing with that boy any more.
But, Dad, why?
You should be playing with kids your own color.
I don't see what skin color has to do with anything.

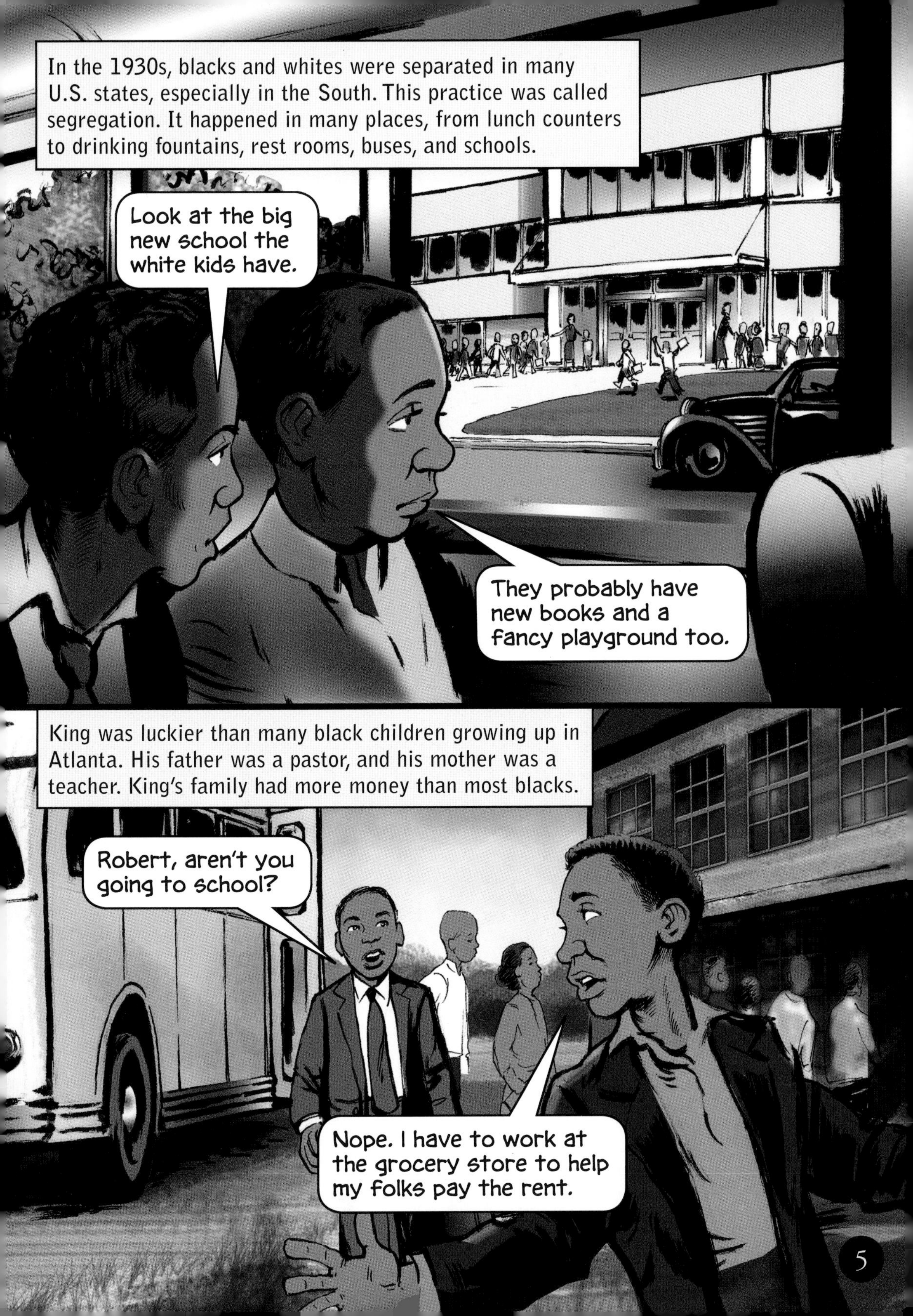
In the 1930s, blacks and whites were separated in many U.S. states, especially in the South. This practice was called segregation. It happened in many places, from lunch counters to drinking fountains, rest rooms, buses, and schools.
Look at the big new school the white kids have.
They probably have new books and a fancy playground too.
King was luckier than many black children growing up in Atlanta. His father was a pastor, and his mother was a teacher. King's family had more money than most blacks.
Robert, aren't you going to school?
Nope. I have to work at the grocery store to help my folks pay the rent.

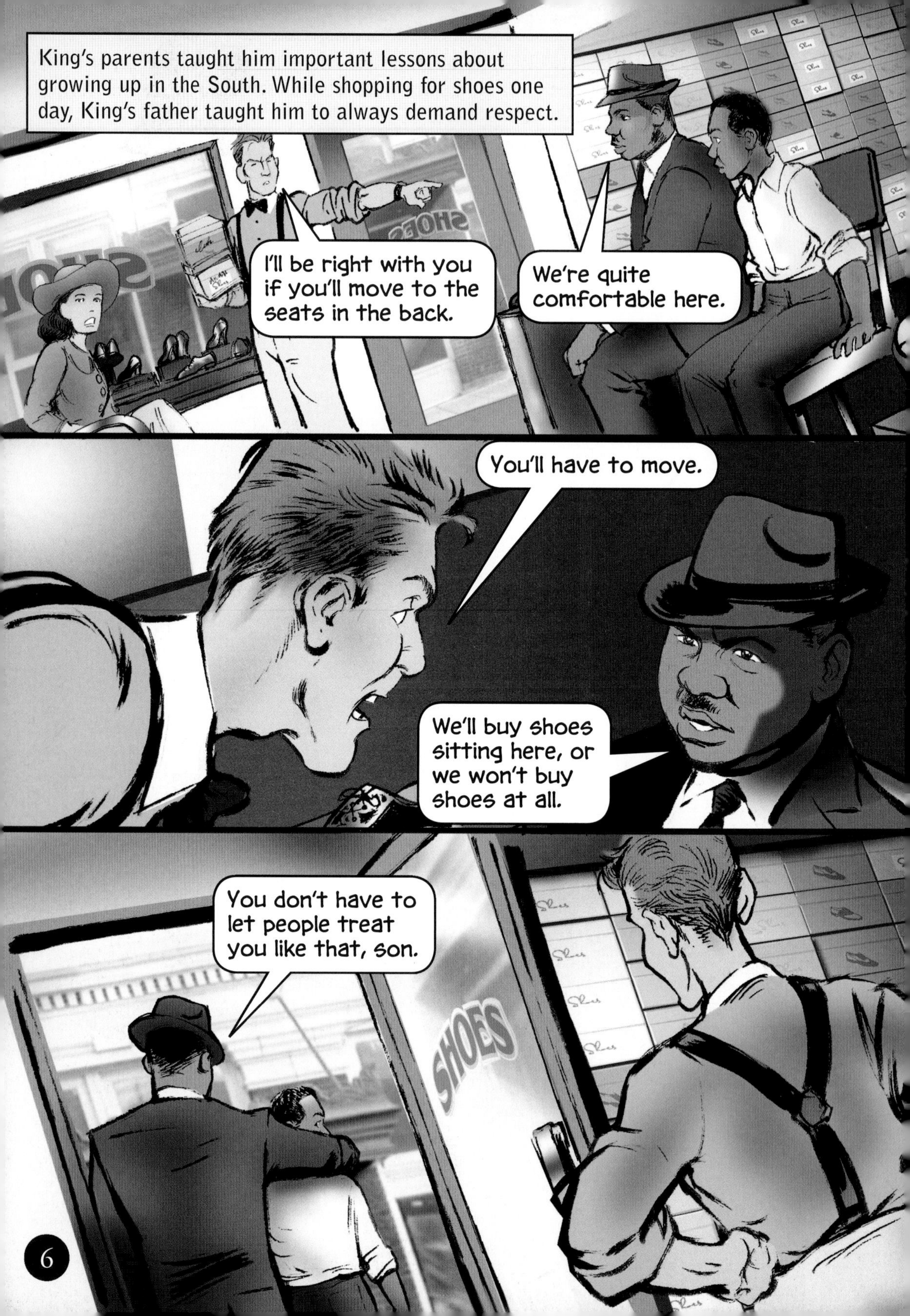
King's parents taught him important lessons about growing up in the South. While shopping for shoes one day, King's father taught him to always demand respect.
I'll be right with you if you'll move to the seats in the back.
We're quite comfortable here.
You'll have to move.
We'll buy shoes sitting here, or we won't buy shoes at all.
You don't have to let people treat you like that, son.
SHOES

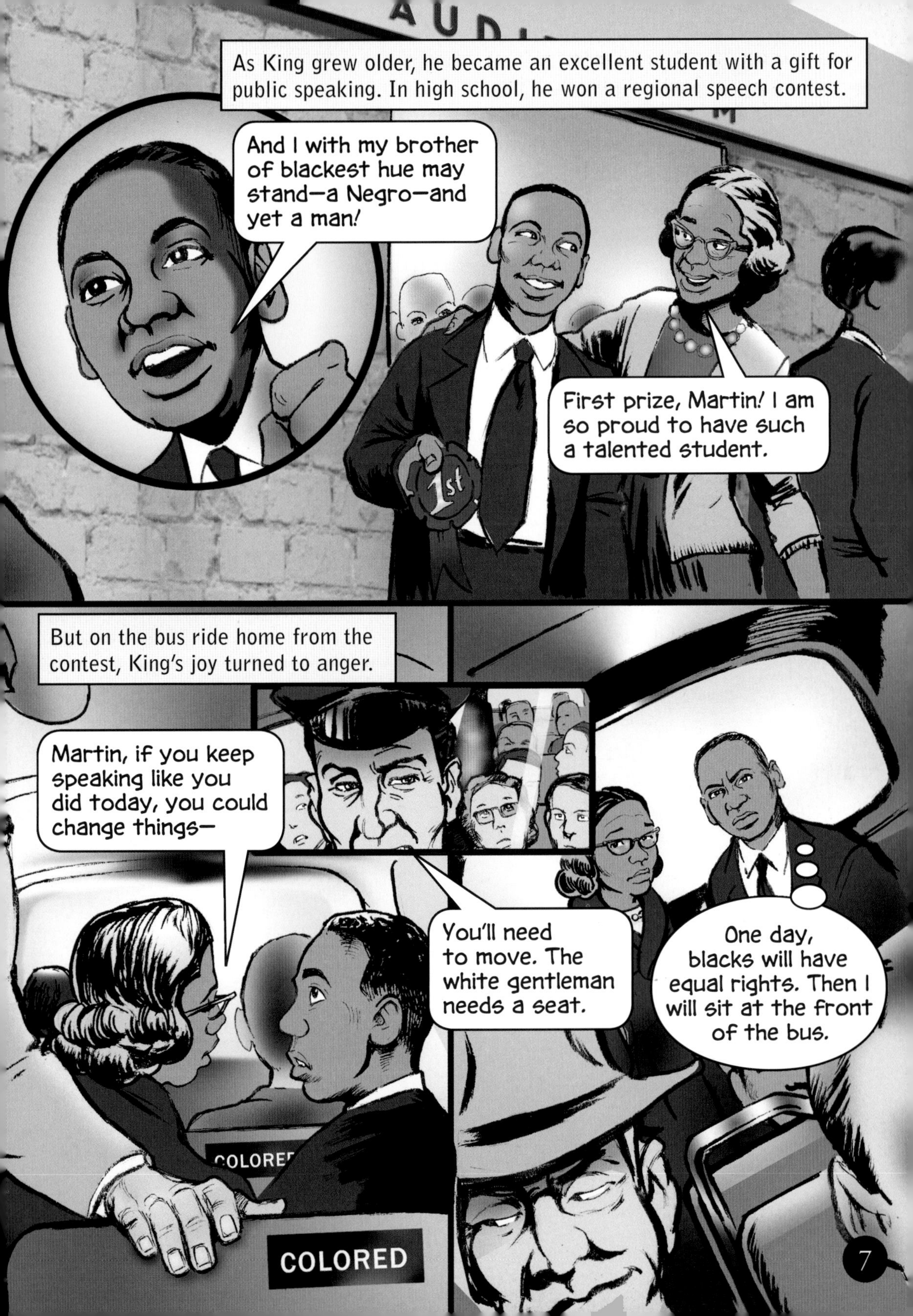

As King grew older, he became an excellent student with a gift for public speaking. In high school, he won a regional speech contest.
And I with my brother of blackest hue may stand—a Negro—and yet a man!
First prize, Martin! I am so proud to have such a talented student.
1st
But on the bus ride home from the contest, King's joy turned to anger.
Martin, if you keep speaking like you did today, you could change things—
You'll need to move. The white gentleman needs a seat.
One day, blacks will have equal rights. Then I will sit at the front of the bus.
COLORED
COLORED

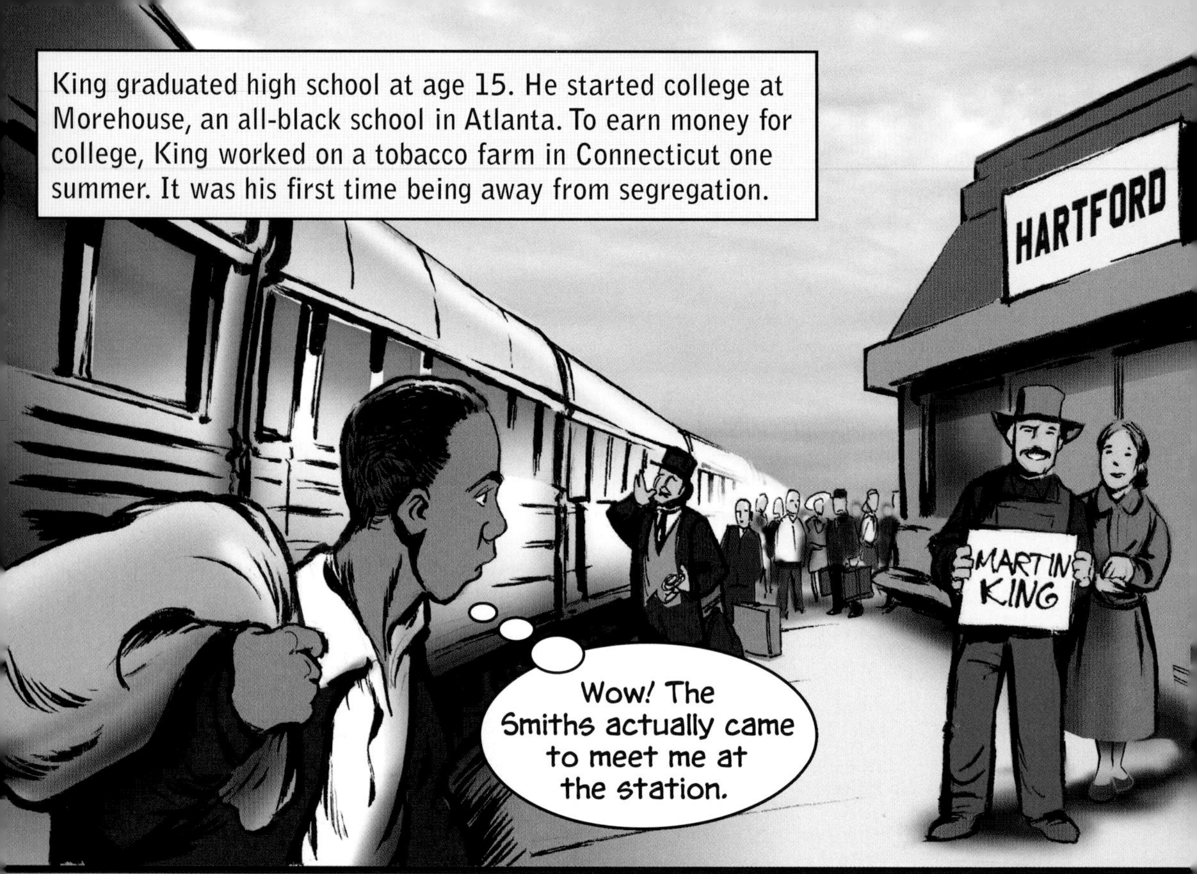
King graduated high school at age 15. He started college at Morehouse, an all-black school in Atlanta. To earn money for college, King worked on a tobacco farm in Connecticut one summer. It was his first time being away from segregation.
HARTFORD
MARTIN KING
Wow! The Smiths actually came to meet me at the station.

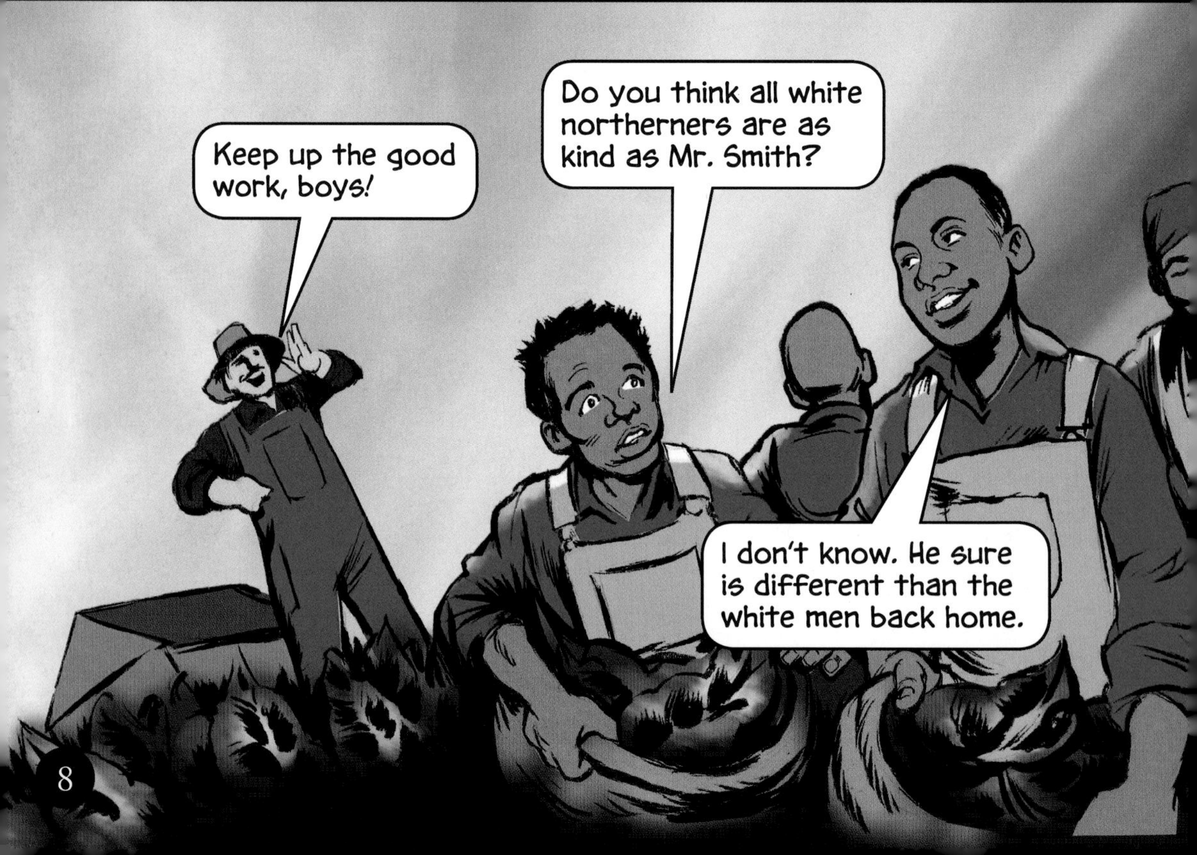
Keep up the good work, boys!
Do you think all white northerners are as kind as Mr. Smith?
I don't know. He sure is different than the white men back home.

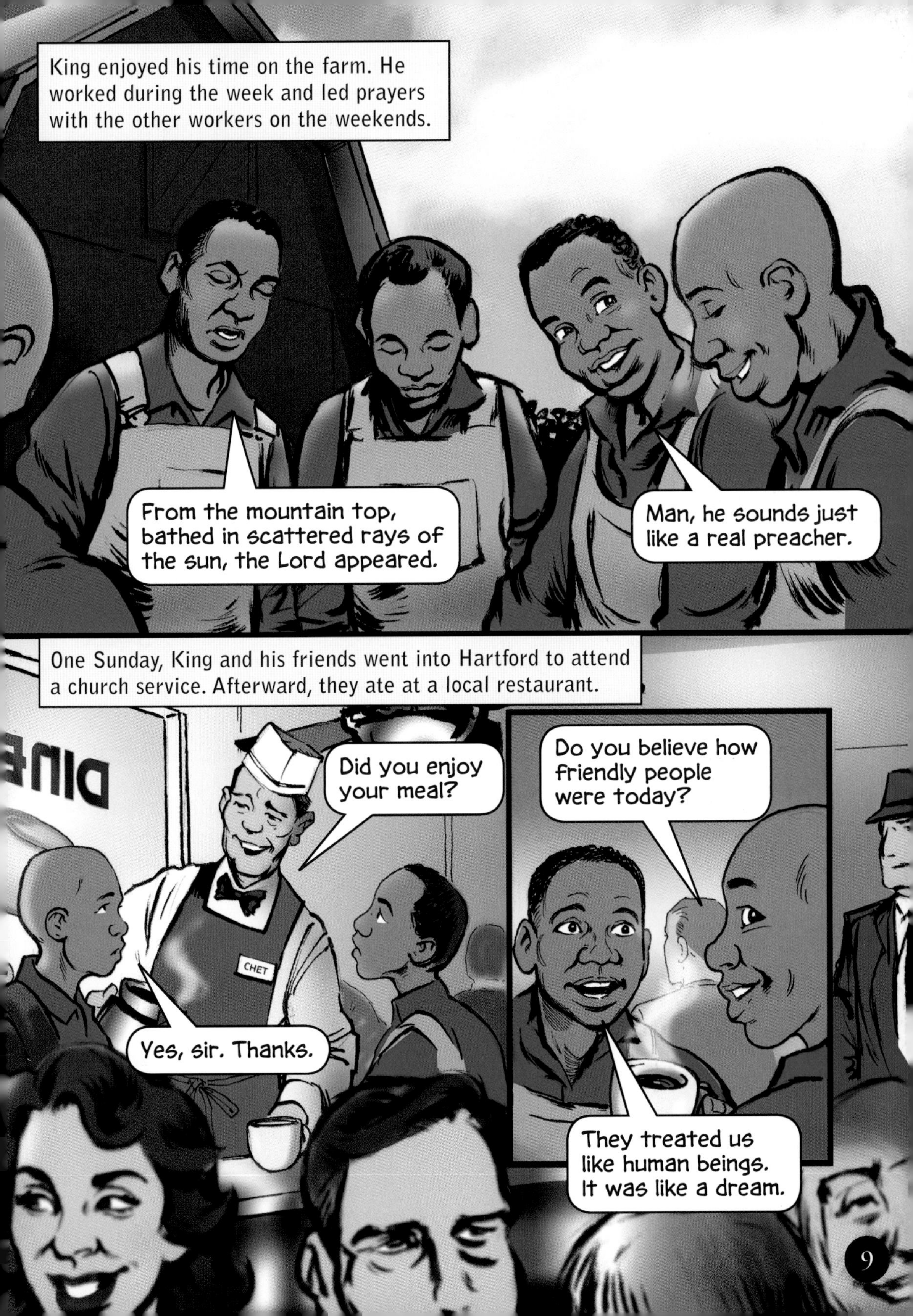
King enjoyed his time on the farm. He worked during the week and led prayers with the other workers on the weekends.
From the mountain top, bathed in scattered rays of the sun, the Lord appeared.
Man, he sounds just like a real preacher.
One Sunday, King and his friends went into Hartford to attend a church service. Afterward, they ate at a local restaurant.
Did you enjoy your meal?
CHET
Yes, sir. Thanks.
Do you believe how friendly people were today?
They treated us like human beings. It was like a dream.

CHAPTER 2

WE SHALL OVERCOME

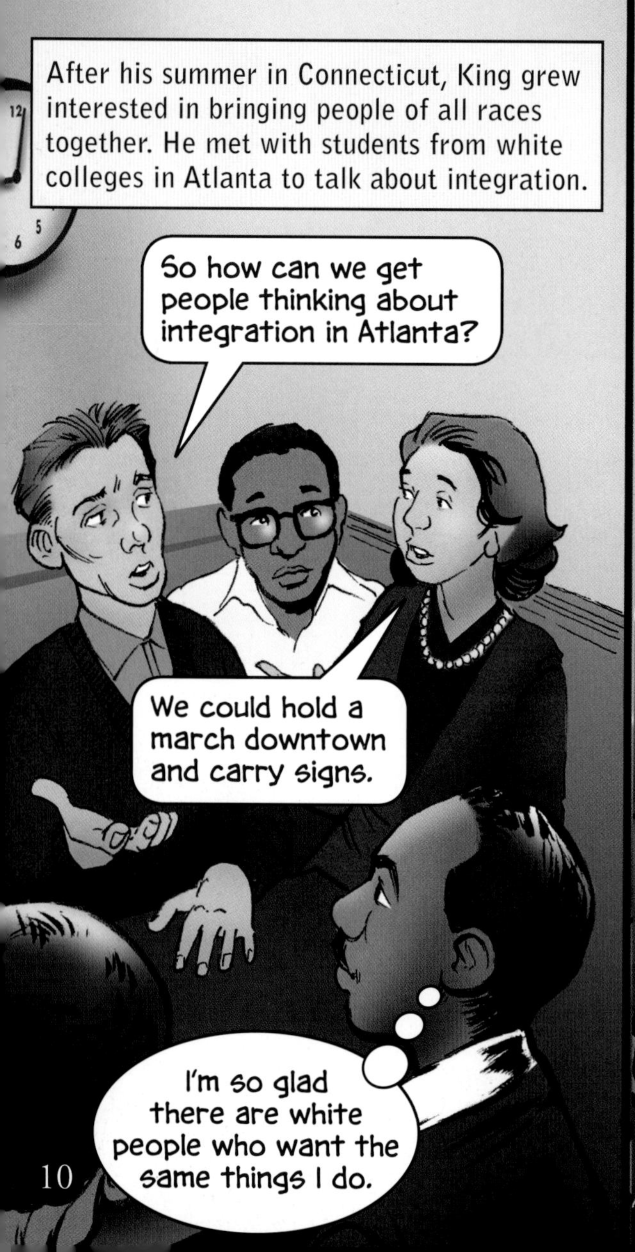

After his summer in Connecticut, King grew interested in bringing people of all races together. He met with students from white colleges in Atlanta to talk about integration.
So how can we get people thinking about integration in Atlanta?
We could hold a march downtown and carry signs.
I'm so glad there are white people who want the same things I do.

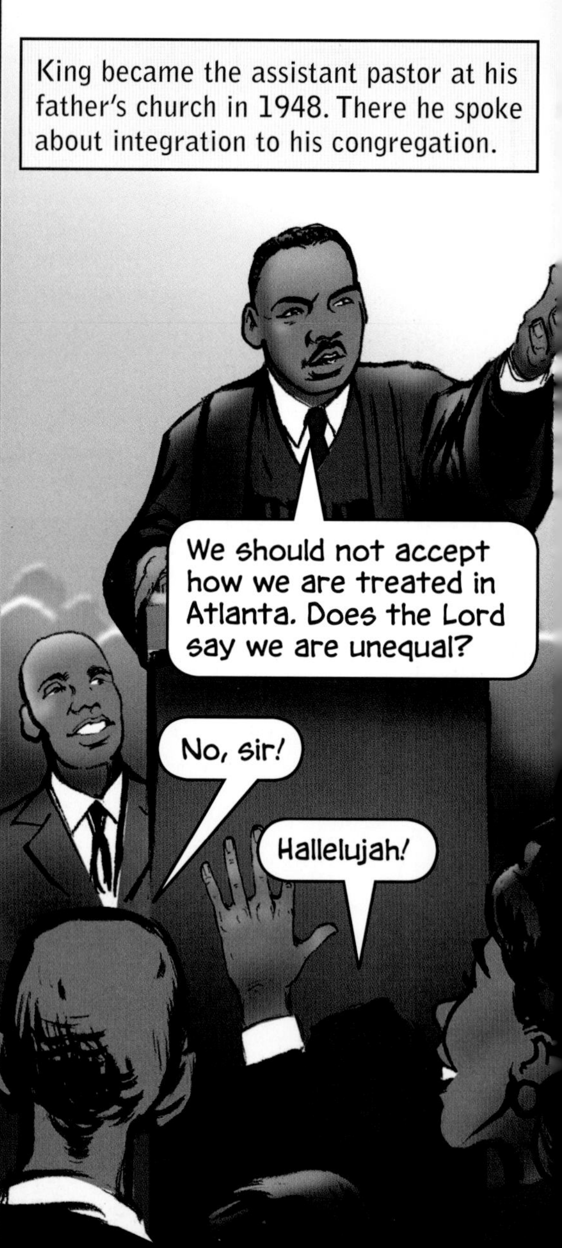

King became the assistant pastor at his father's church in 1948. There he spoke about integration to his congregation.
We should not accept how we are treated in Atlanta. Does the Lord say we are unequal?
No, sir!
Hallelujah!

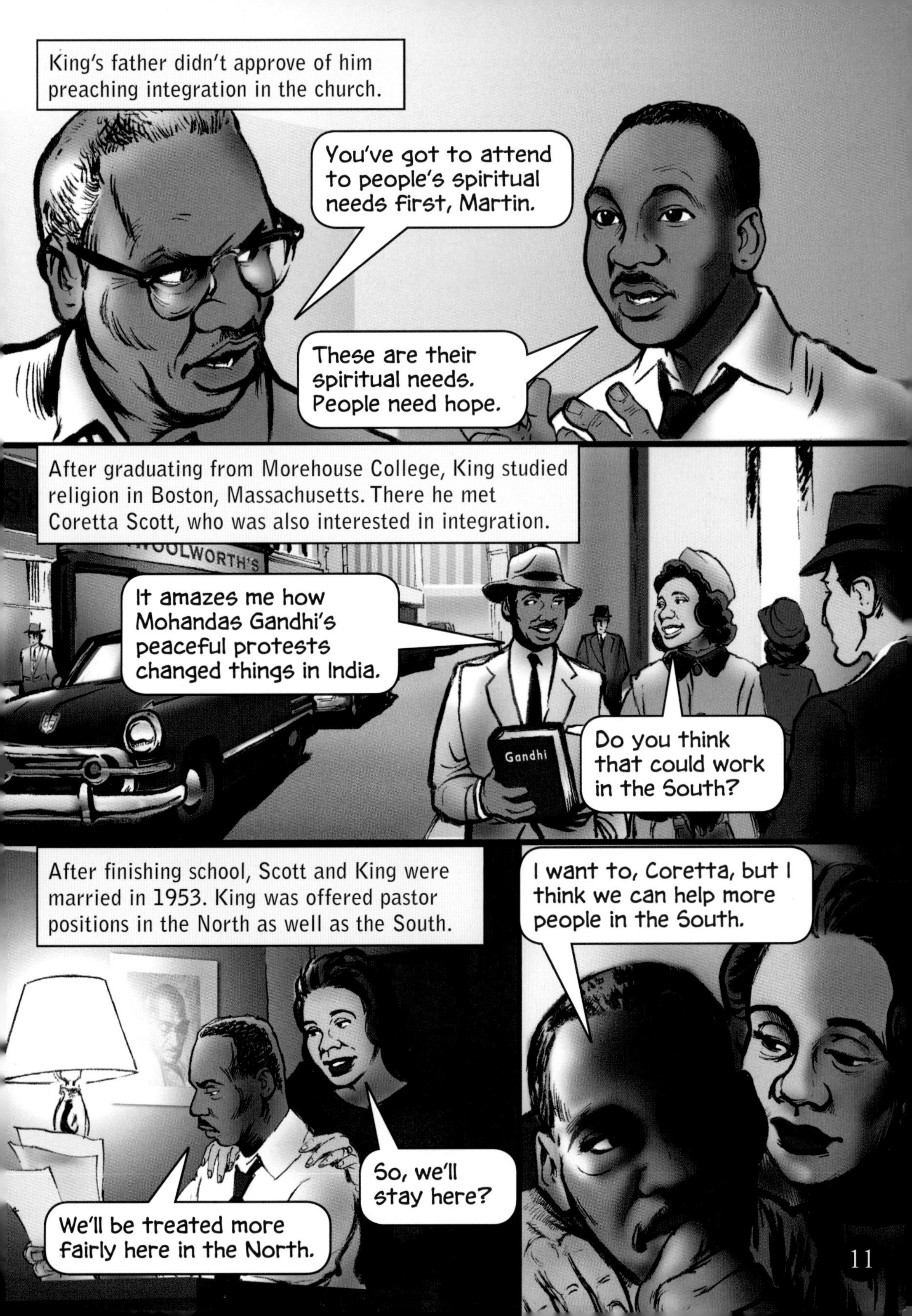
King's father didn't approve of him preaching integration in the church.
You've got to attend to people's spiritual needs first, Martin.
These are their spiritual needs. People need hope.
After graduating from Morehouse College, King studied religion in Boston, Massachusetts. There he met Coretta Scott, who was also interested in integration.
WOOLWORTH'S
It amazes me how Mohandas Gandhi's peaceful protests changed things in India.
Gandhi
Do you think that could work in the South?
After finishing school, Scott and King were married in 1953. King was offered pastor positions in the North as well as the South.
We'll be treated more fairly here in the North.
So, we'll stay here?
I want to, Coretta, but I think we can help more people in the South.

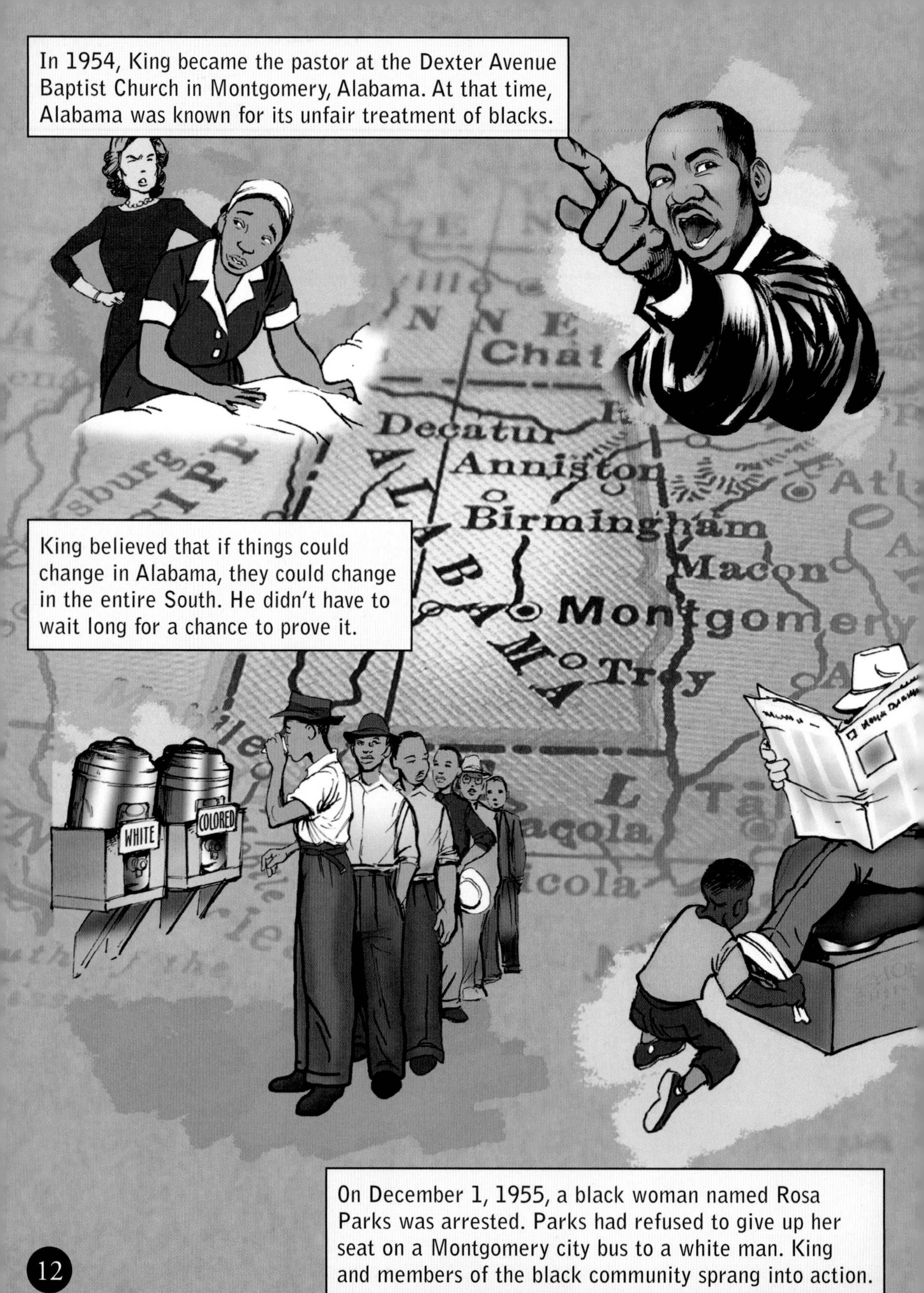
In 1954, King became the pastor at the Dexter Avenue Baptist Church in Montgomery, Alabama. At that time, Alabama was known for its unfair treatment of blacks.
Decatur
Anniston
Birmingham
Macon
Montgomery
Troy
ALABAMA
King believed that if things could change in Alabama, they could change in the entire South. He didn't have to wait long for a chance to prove it.
WHITE
COLORED
On December 1, 1955, a black woman named Rosa Parks was arrested. Parks had refused to give up her seat on a Montgomery city bus to a white man. King and members of the black community sprang into action.

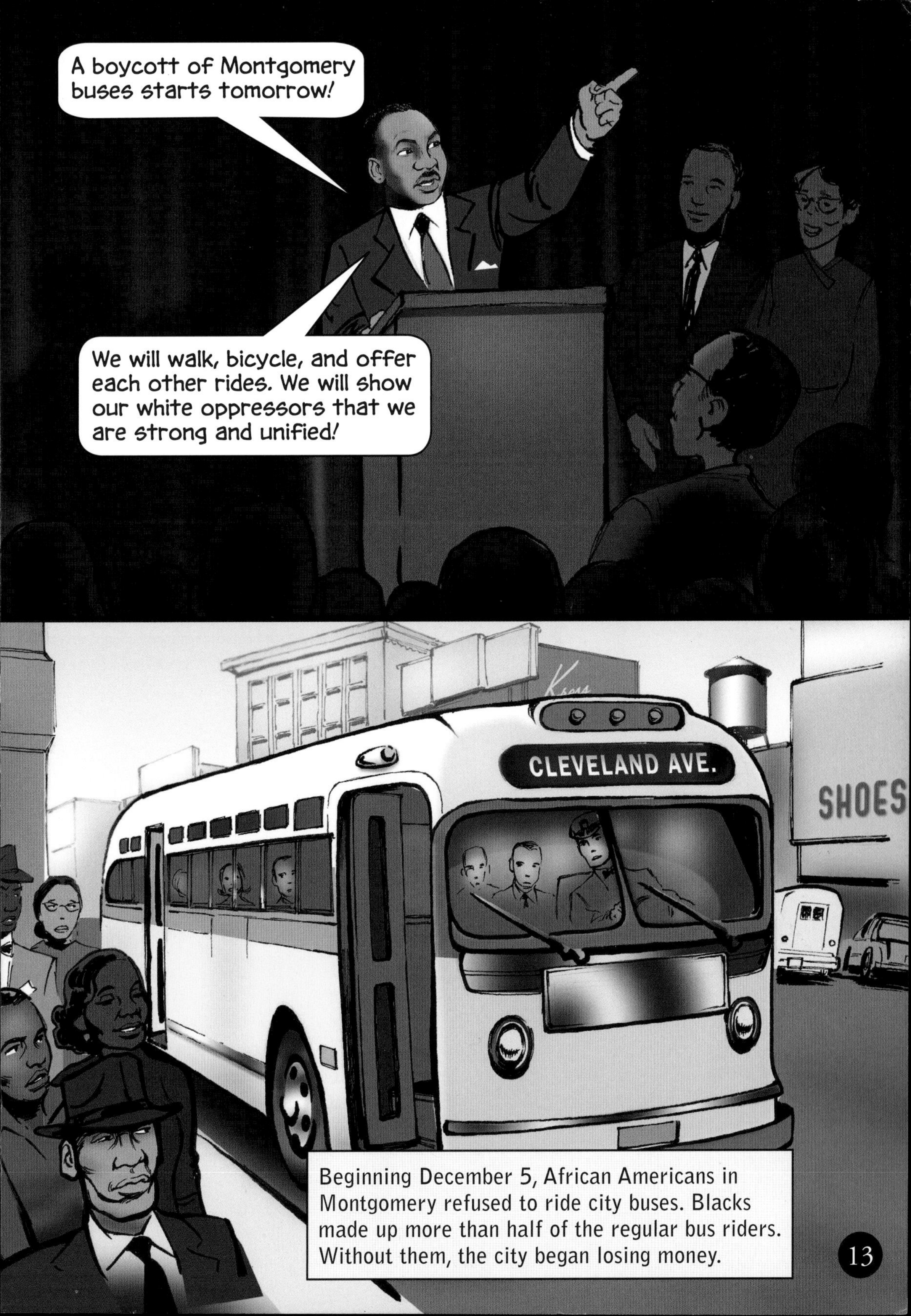
A boycott of Montgomery buses starts tomorrow!
We will walk, bicycle, and offer each other rides. We will show our white oppressors that we are strong and unified!
CLEVELAND AVE.
SHOES
Beginning December 5, African Americans in Montgomery refused to ride city buses. Blacks made up more than half of the regular bus riders. Without them, the city began losing money.

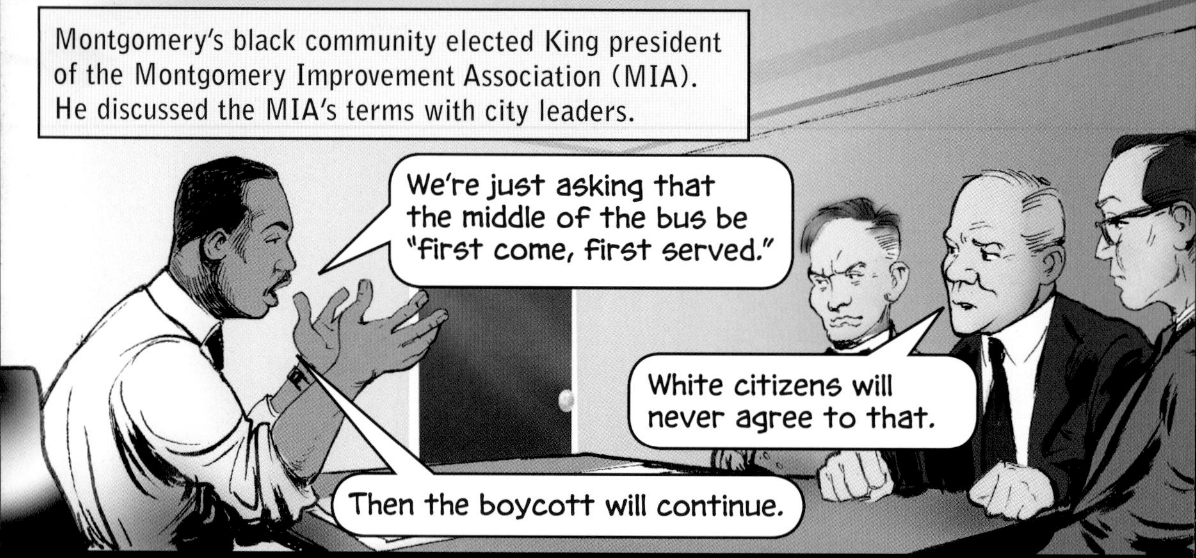
Montgomery's black community elected King president of the Montgomery Improvement Association (MIA). He discussed the MIA's terms with city leaders.
We're just asking that the middle of the bus be "first come, first served."
White citizens will never agree to that.
Then the boycott will continue.

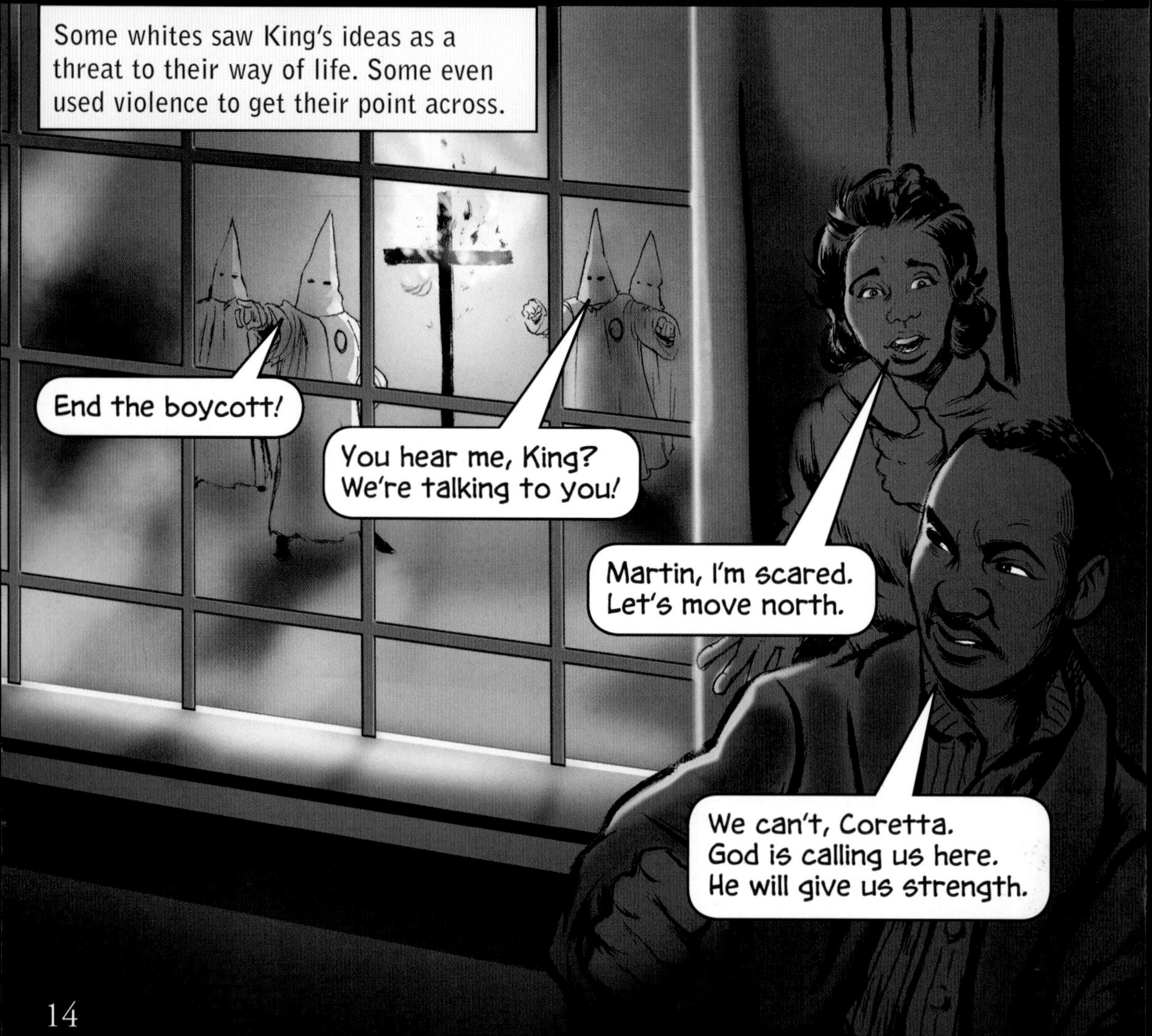
Some whites saw King's ideas as a threat to their way of life. Some even used violence to get their point across.
End the boycott!
You hear me, King? We're talking to you!
Martin, I'm scared. Let's move north.
We can't, Coretta. God is calling us here. He will give us strength.

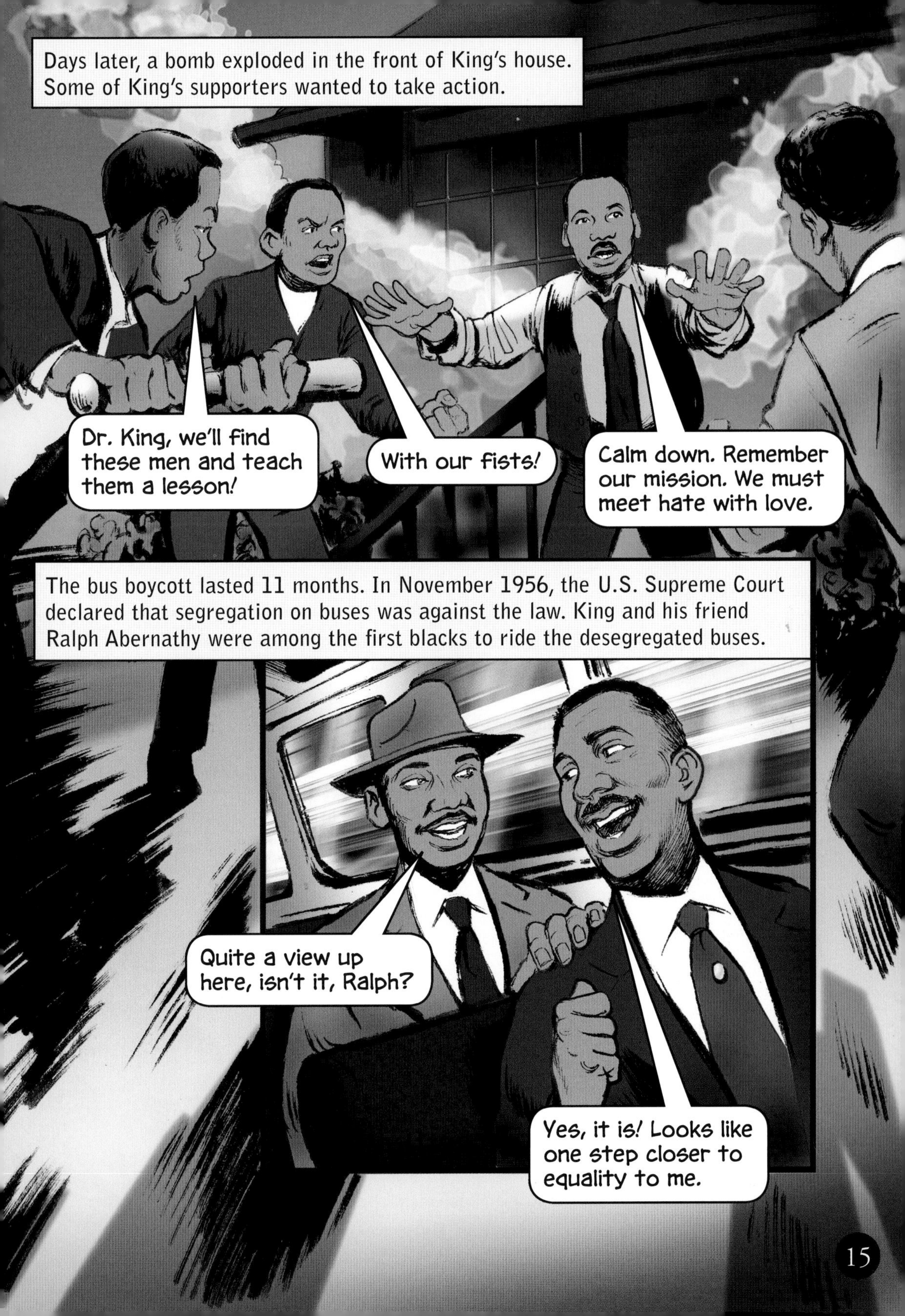

Days later, a bomb exploded in the front of King's house. Some of King's supporters wanted to take action.
Dr. King, we'll find these men and teach them a lesson!
With our fists!
Calm down. Remember our mission. We must meet hate with love.
The bus boycott lasted 11 months. In November 1956, the U.S. Supreme Court declared that segregation on buses was against the law. King and his friend Ralph Abernathy were among the first blacks to ride the desegregated buses.
Quite a view up here, isn't it, Ralph?
Yes, it is! Looks like one step closer to equality to me.

CHAPTER 3

DR. KING'S DREAM

After King's work on the Montgomery bus boycott, people around the world knew the name Martin Luther King Jr.

Reverend King ...eak at

The Boston Glo...

CIVIL RIGHTS LEA...

LOOK

The F...

KING CALLS FOR EQUAL

King became president of the Southern Christian Leadership Conference (SCLC), an organization of southern pastors who worked for civil rights.

TIME
THE WEEKLY NEWSMAGAZINE

King was now the spokesperson for the civil rights movement. He was one of many people who hoped to get African Americans equal rights.

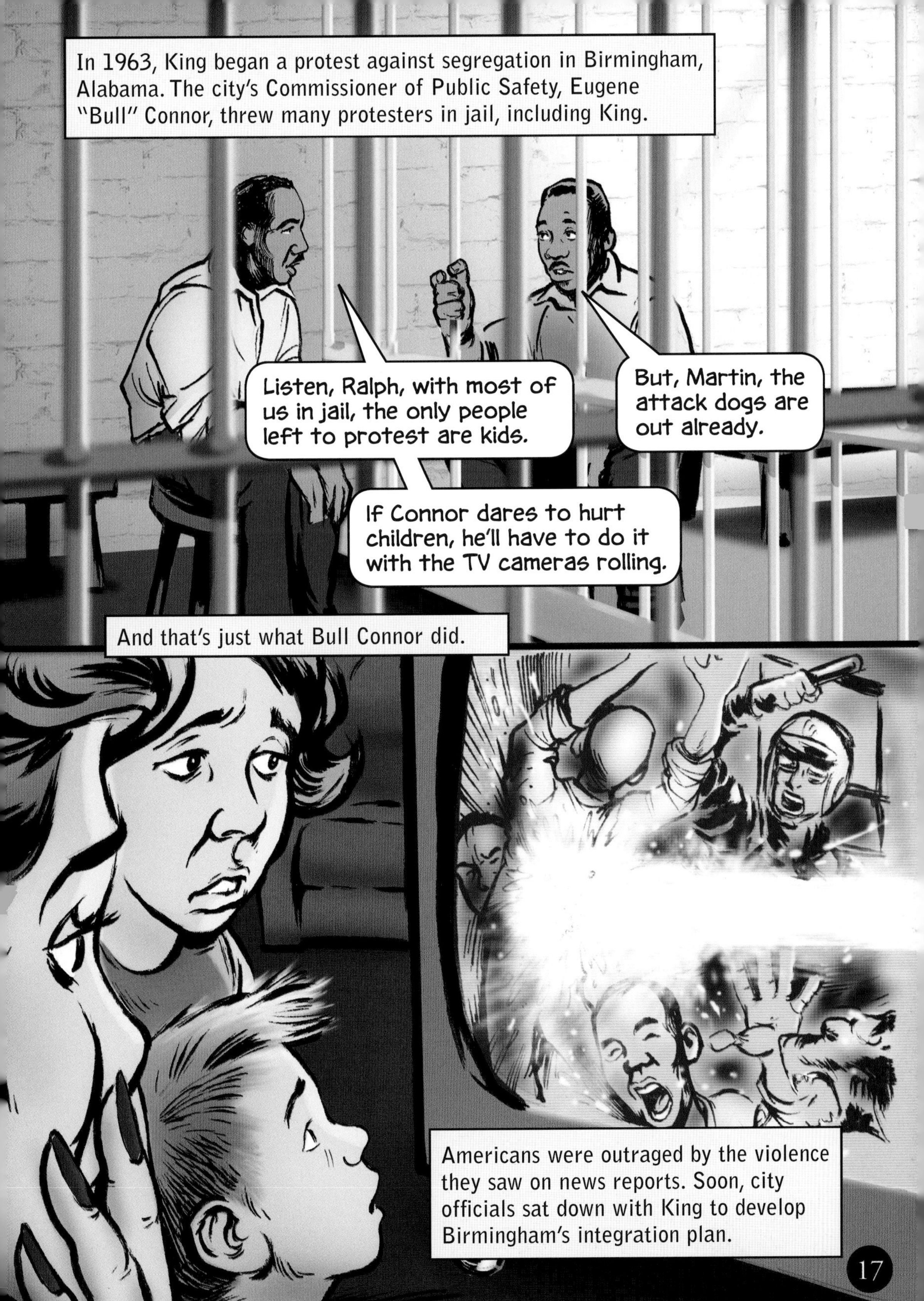
In 1963, King began a protest against segregation in Birmingham, Alabama. The city's Commissioner of Public Safety, Eugene "Bull" Connor, threw many protesters in jail, including King.
Listen, Ralph, with most of us in jail, the only people left to protest are kids.
But, Martin, the attack dogs are out already.
If Connor dares to hurt children, he'll have to do it with the TV cameras rolling.
And that's just what Bull Connor did.
Americans were outraged by the violence they saw on news reports. Soon, city officials sat down with King to develop Birmingham's integration plan.

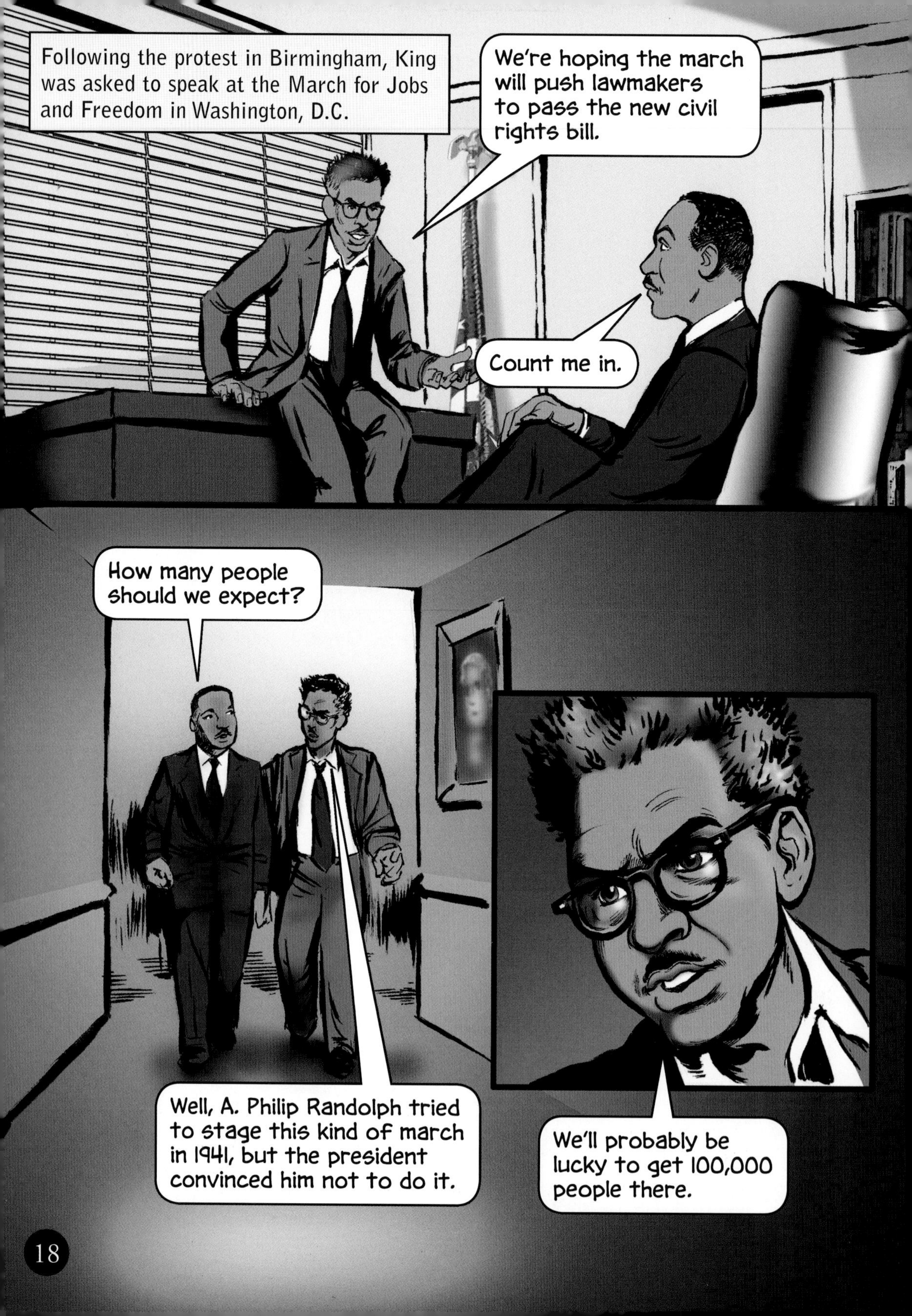
Following the protest in Birmingham, King was asked to speak at the March for Jobs and Freedom in Washington, D.C.
We're hoping the march will push lawmakers to pass the new civil rights bill.
Count me in.
How many people should we expect?
Well, A. Philip Randolph tried to stage this kind of march in 1941, but the president convinced him not to do it.
We'll probably be lucky to get 100,000 people there.

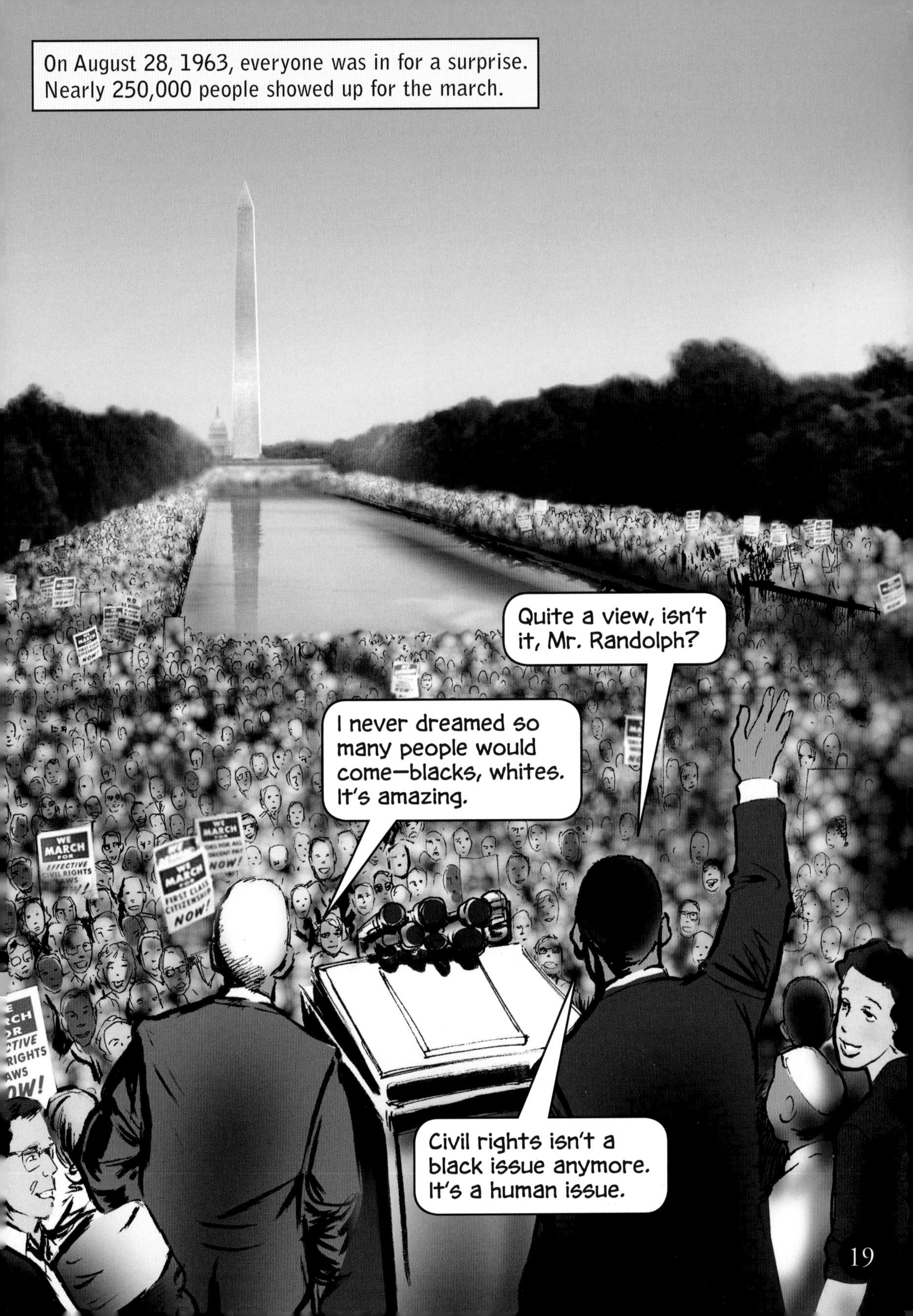
On August 28, 1963, everyone was in for a surprise. Nearly 250,000 people showed up for the march.
Quite a view, isn't it, Mr. Randolph?
I never dreamed so many people would come—blacks, whites. It's amazing.
Civil rights isn't a black issue anymore. It's a human issue.
WE MARCH FOR FIRST CLASS CITIZENSHIP NOW!

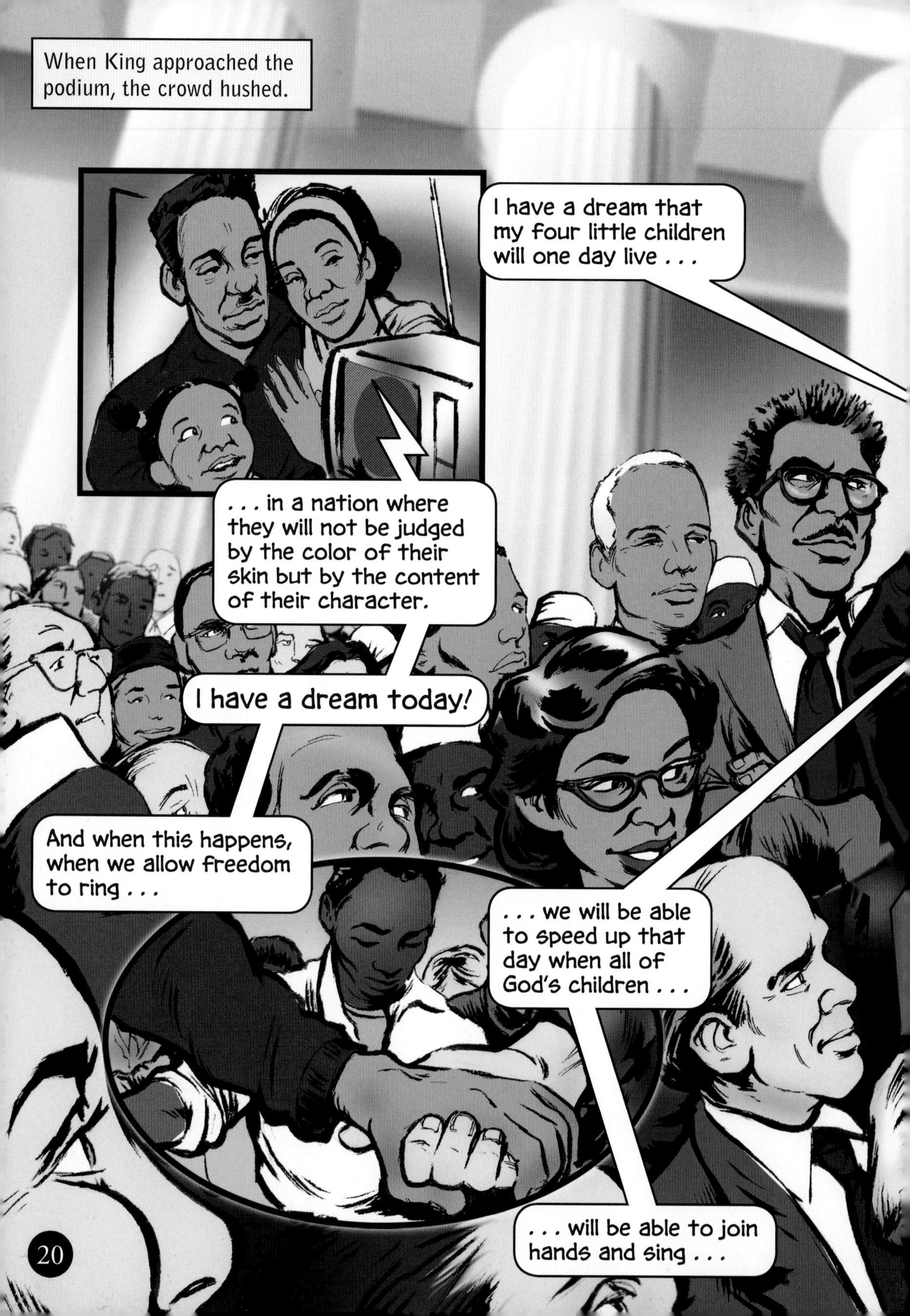
When King approached the podium, the crowd hushed.
I have a dream that my four little children will one day live . . .
. . . in a nation where they will not be judged by the color of their skin but by the content of their character.
I have a dream today!
And when this happens, when we allow freedom to ring . . .
. . . we will be able to speed up that day when all of God's children . . .
. . . will be able to join hands and sing . . .

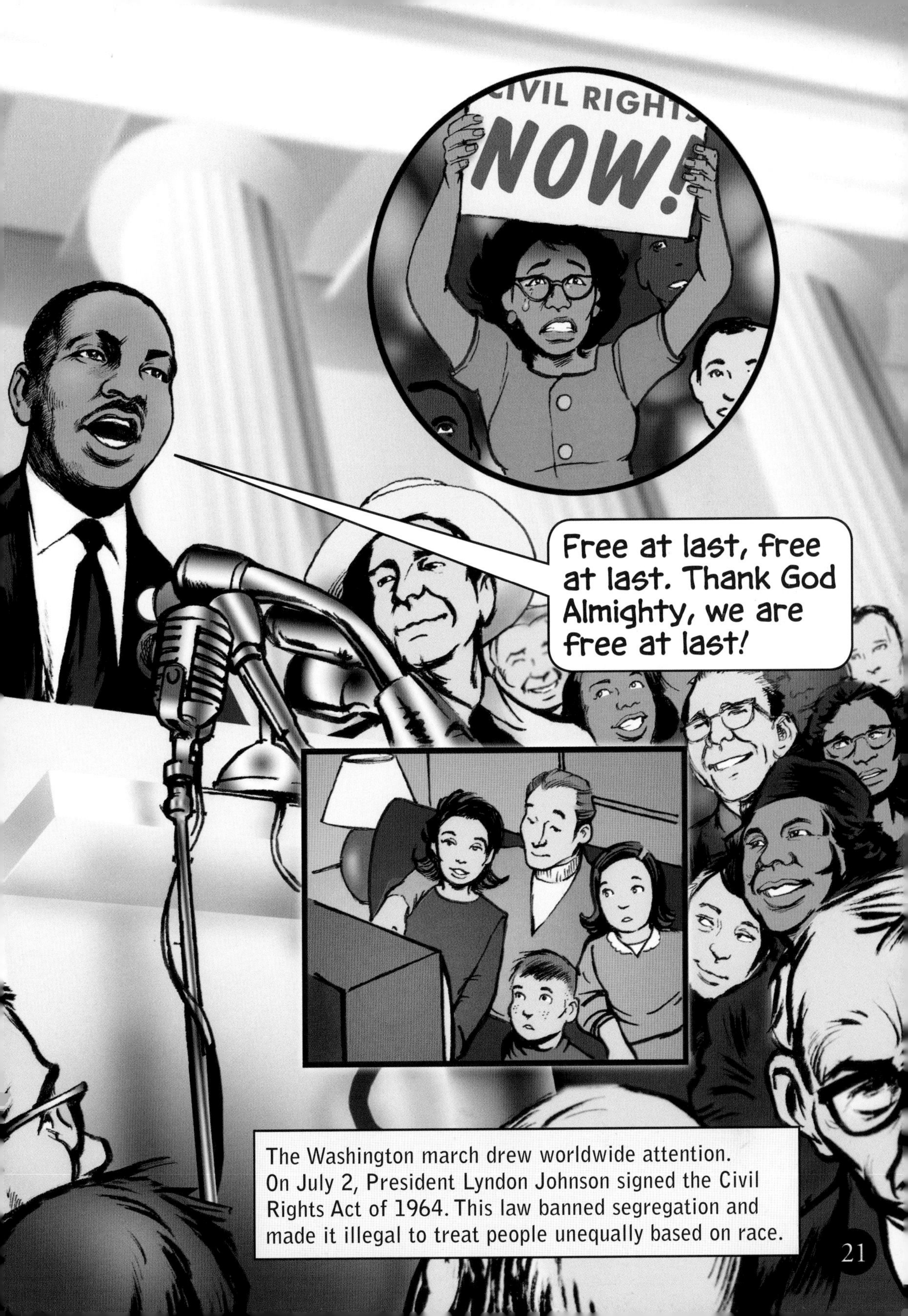
NOW!
Free at last, free at last. Thank God Almighty, we are free at last!
The Washington march drew worldwide attention. On July 2, President Lyndon Johnson signed the Civil Rights Act of 1964. This law banned segregation and made it illegal to treat people unequally based on race.

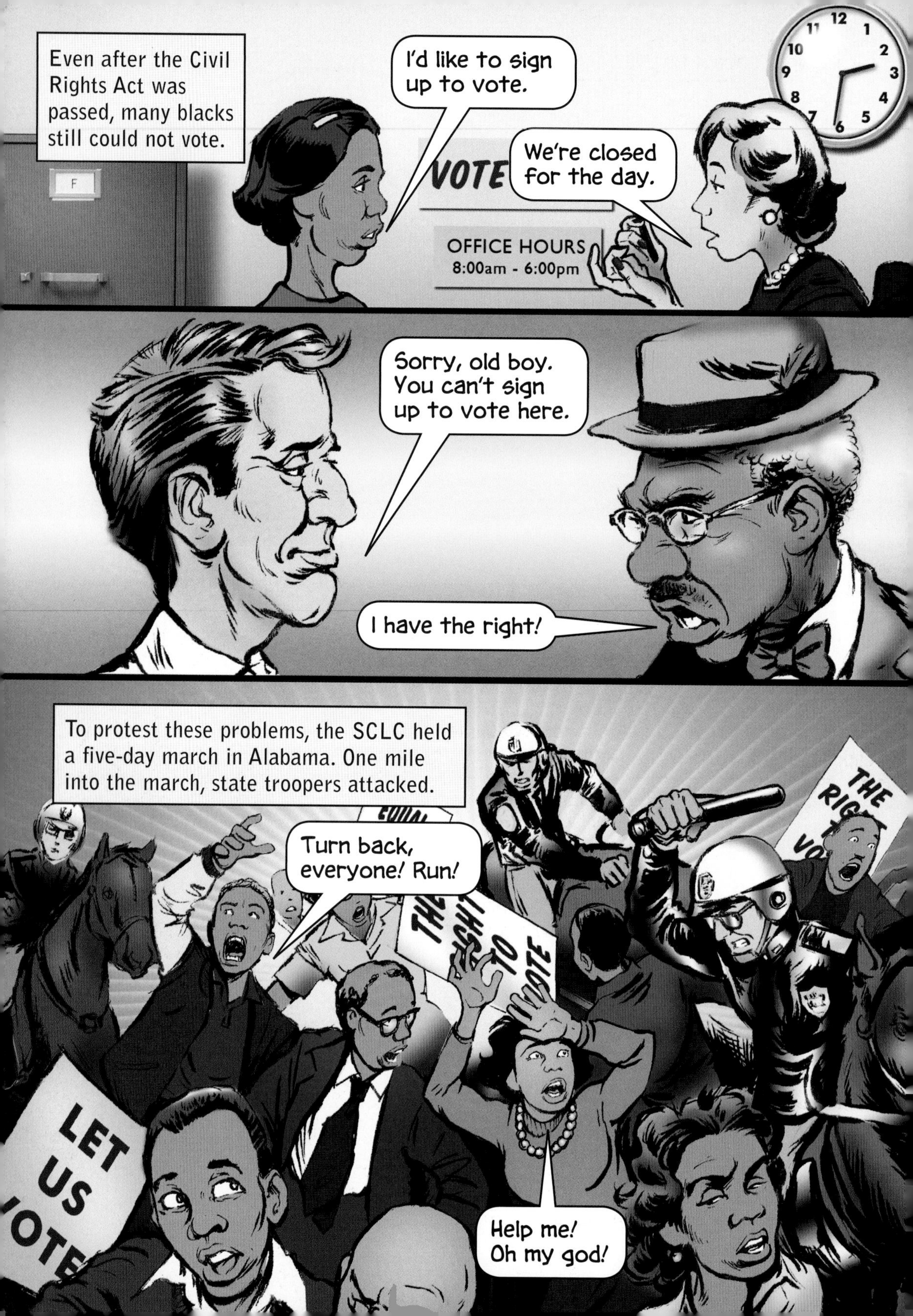
Even after the Civil Rights Act was passed, many blacks still could not vote.
I'd like to sign up to vote.
VOTE
We're closed for the day.
OFFICE HOURS
8:00am - 6:00pm
Sorry, old boy. You can't sign up to vote here.
I have the right!
To protest these problems, the SCLC held a five-day march in Alabama. One mile into the march, state troopers attacked.
Turn back, everyone! Run!
LET US
Help me! Oh my god!

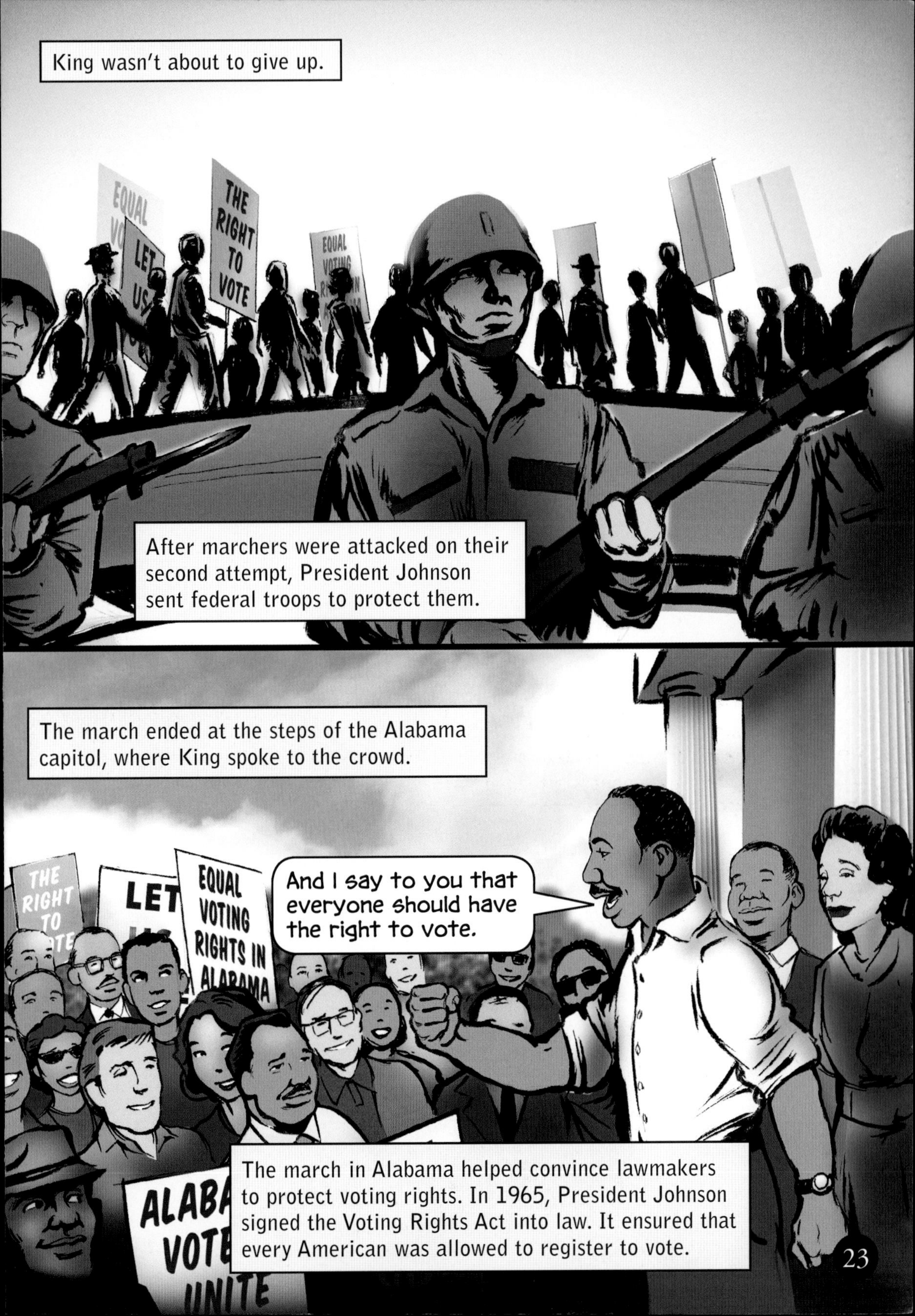
King wasn't about to give up.
THE RIGHT TO VOTE
EQUAL
After marchers were attacked on their second attempt, President Johnson sent federal troops to protect them.
The march ended at the steps of the Alabama capitol, where King spoke to the crowd.
THE RIGHT TO
LET
EQUAL VOTING RIGHTS IN
And I say to you that everyone should have the right to vote.
The march in Alabama helped convince lawmakers to protect voting rights. In 1965, President Johnson signed the Voting Rights Act into law. It ensured that every American was allowed to register to vote.

CHAPTER 4

THE DREAM LIVES ON

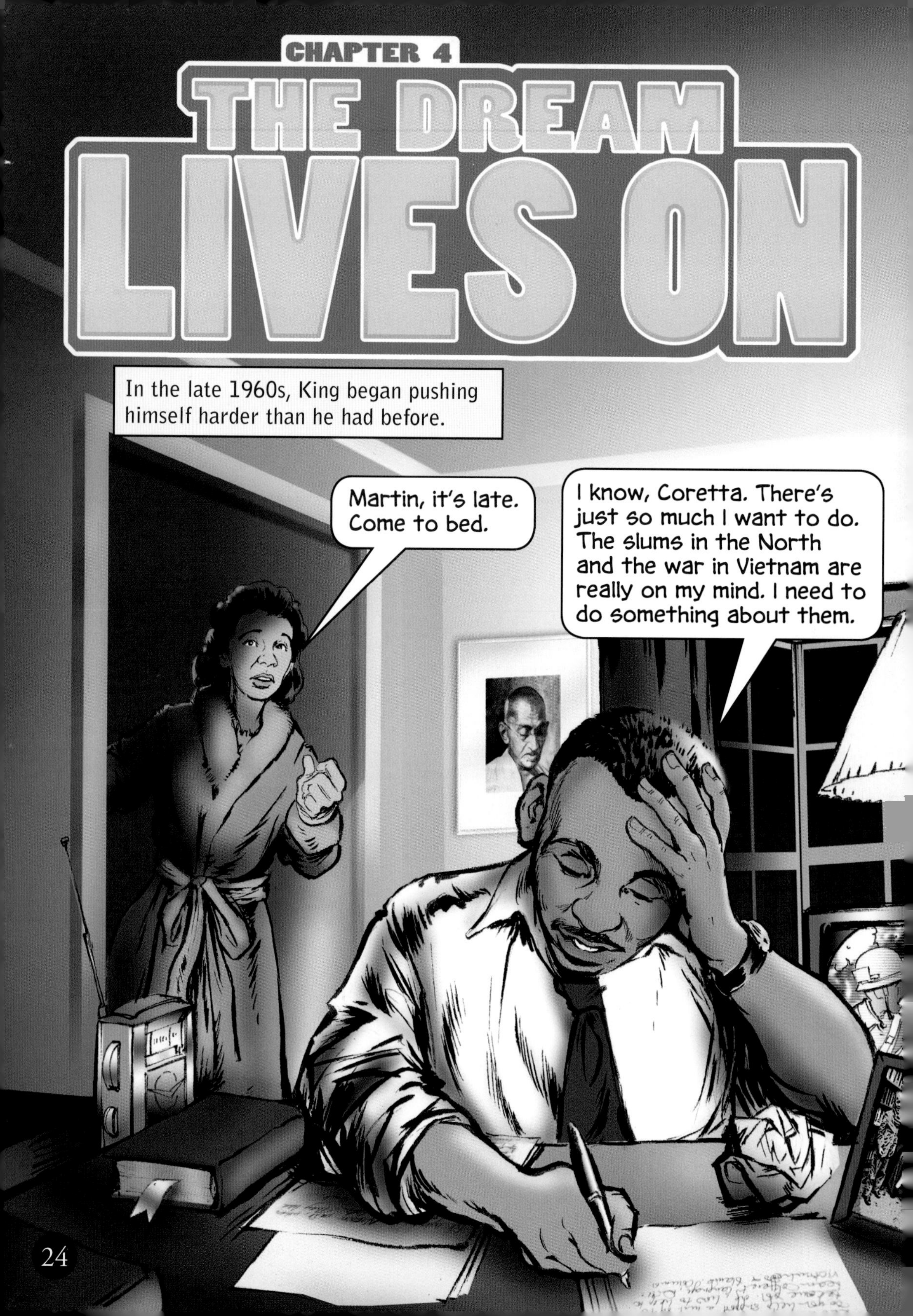
In the late 1960s, King began pushing himself harder than he had before.
Martin, it's late. Come to bed.
I know, Coretta. There's just so much I want to do. The slums in the North and the war in Vietnam are really on my mind. I need to do something about them.

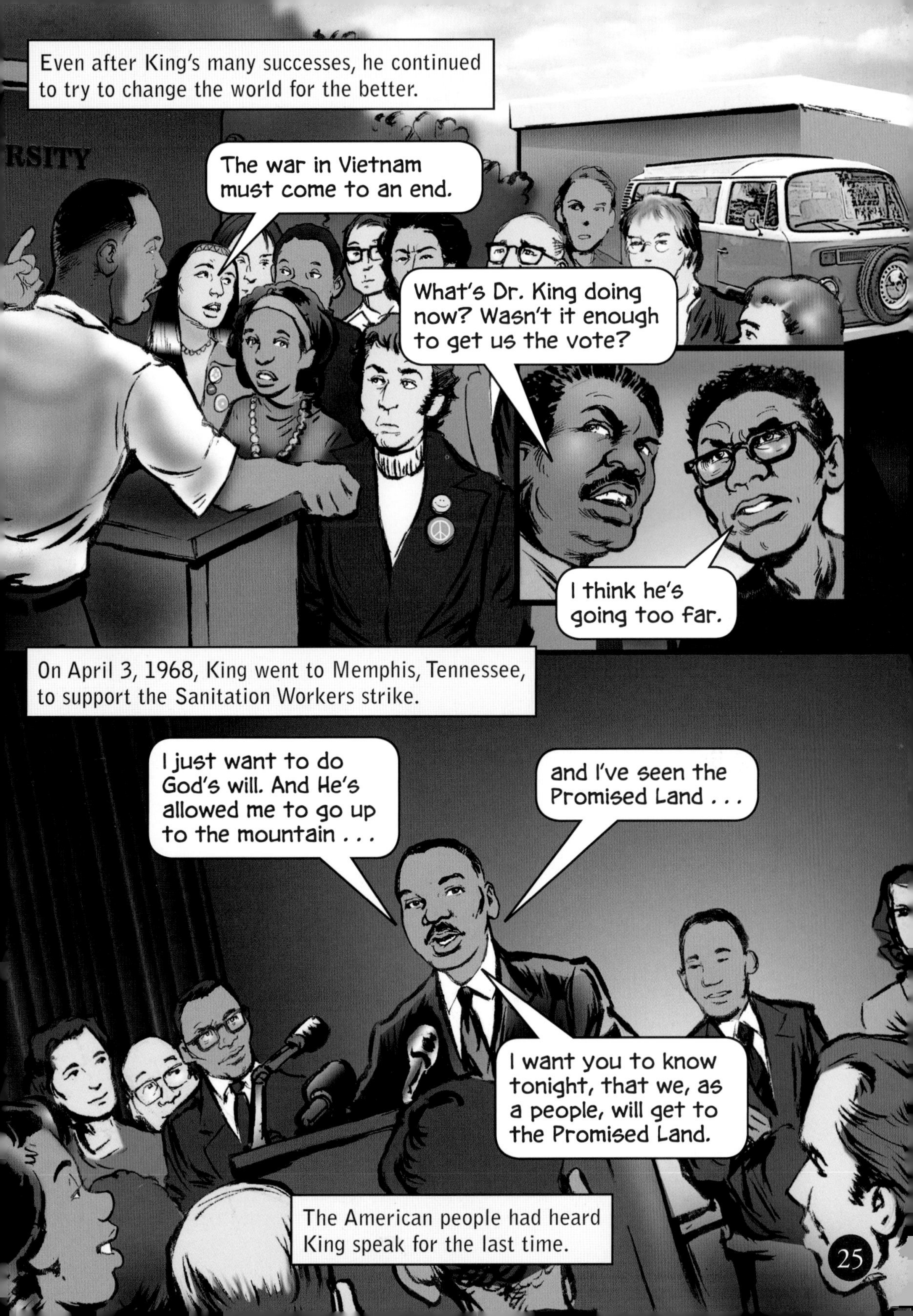

Even after King's many successes, he continued to try to change the world for the better.
RSITY
The war in Vietnam must come to an end.
What's Dr. King doing now? Wasn't it enough to get us the vote?
I think he's going too far.
On April 3, 1968, King went to Memphis, Tennessee, to support the Sanitation Workers strike.
I just want to do God's will. And He's allowed me to go up to the mountain . . .
and I've seen the Promised Land . . .
I want you to know tonight, that we, as a people, will get to the Promised Land.
The American people had heard King speak for the last time.

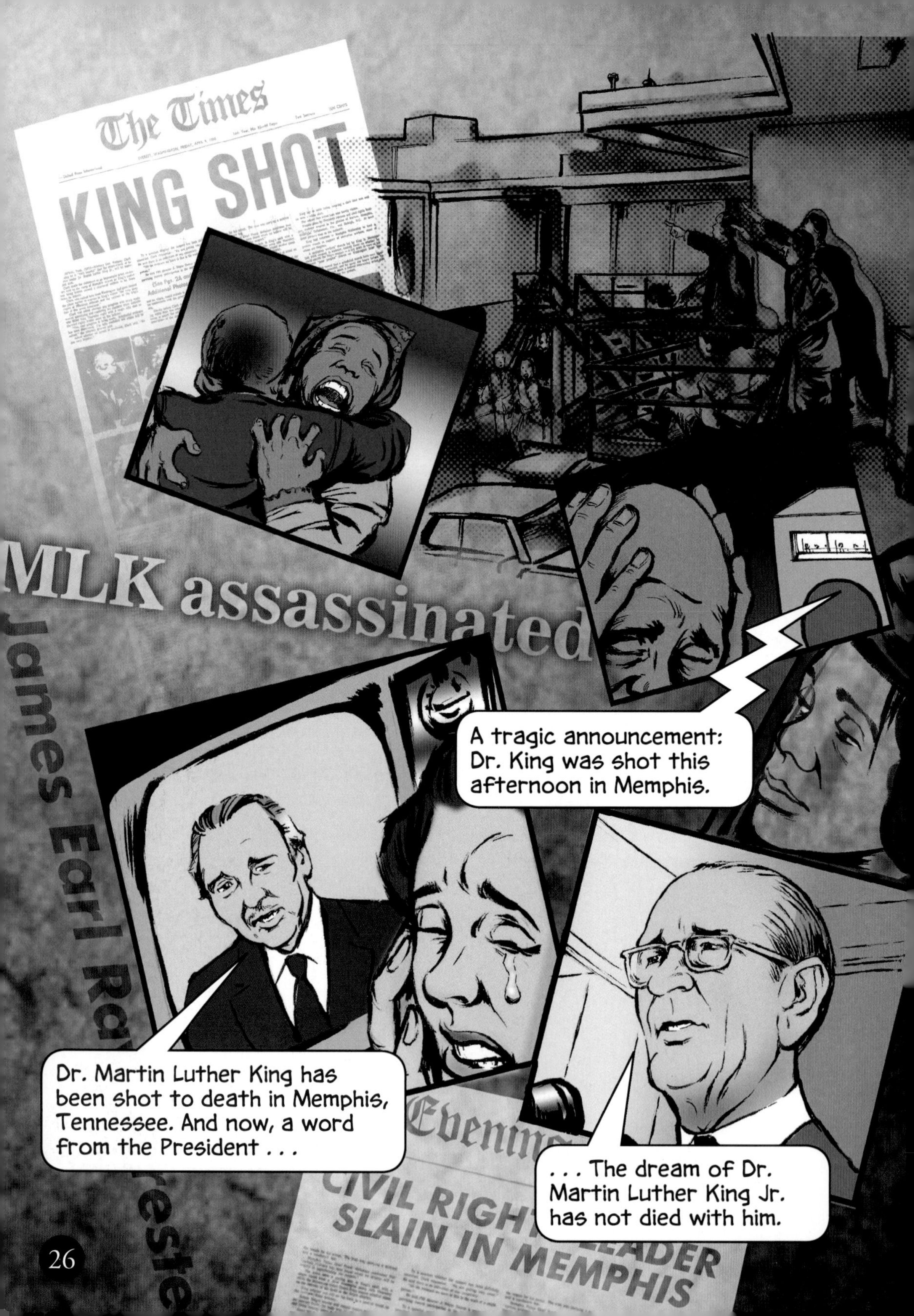
The Times
KING SHOT
MLK assassinated
A tragic announcement: Dr. King was shot this afternoon in Memphis.
Dr. Martin Luther King has been shot to death in Memphis, Tennessee. And now, a word from the President . . .
. . . The dream of Dr. Martin Luther King Jr. has not died with him.
SLAIN IN MEMPHIS

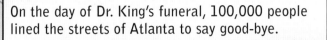

On the day of Dr. King's funeral, 100,000 people lined the streets of Atlanta to say good-bye.

And 50,000 more marched behind his coffin. They followed him, just as they had when he was alive. King was gone, but his dream has lived on.

DR. MARTIN LUTHER KING JR.

- Martin Luther King Jr. was born January 15, 1929, in Atlanta, Georgia. He died April 4, 1968.

- King finished high school when he was only 15. A motivated student, he skipped two grades. Unfortunately, his education at a blacks-only school did not prepare him well for college. King struggled to keep up during his first year at Morehouse College.

- King and his wife, Coretta Scott King, had four children: Yolanda, Martin Luther III, Dexter, and Bernice.

- In 1957, King's first year as spokesperson for the civil rights movement, he traveled around the world delivering speeches. He traveled 780,000 miles that year.

- In 1959, King traveled to India to visit the birthplace of Mohandas Gandhi. Gandhi used nonviolent protests to gain equal rights for the people of India. King was inspired to use peaceful protest after studying Gandhi's work.

- In 1964, King received one of the most important honors in the world, the Nobel Peace Prize. The award recognized his use of nonviolent protest to change laws.

- While King enjoyed successes in his lifetime, he also suffered failures. Toward the end of his career, King tried to draw attention to slum conditions in big cities like Chicago, Illinois. Some African Americans didn't think that King's nonviolent protests would work in the larger northern cities. After being attacked and facing many arguments, King returned to the South to spread his message.

- King's birthday is a national holiday in the United States. People celebrate and honor the holiday on the third Monday in January.

- King's gravestone is engraved with the words "Free at last. Free at last. Thank God Almighty, I'm Free at last."

GLOSSARY

boycott (BOI-kot)—to refuse to take part in something as a way of making a protest

illegal (ill-LEE-guhl)—against the law

integration (in-tuh-GRAY-shuhn)—the practice of including people of all races in schools and other public places

protest (PROH-test)—a demonstration against something

segregation (seg-ruh-GAY-shuhn)—the act of keeping people or groups apart from one another

INTERNET SITES

FactHound offers a safe, fun way to find Internet sites related to this book. All of the sites on FactHound have been researched by our staff.

Here's how:
1. Visit *www.facthound.com*
2. Choose your grade level.
3. Type in this book ID **0736864989** for age-appropriate sites. You may also browse subjects by clicking on letters, or by clicking on pictures and words.
4. Click on the **Fetch It** button.

FactHound will fetch the best sites for you!

READ MORE

Feeney, Kathy. *Martin Luther King, Jr.* Photo-illustrated Biographies. Mankato, Minn.: Bridgestone Books, 2002.

Myers, Walter Dean. *I've Seen the Promised Land. The Life of Dr. Martin Luther King, Jr.* New York: HarperCollins, 2004.

Nettleton, Pamela Hill. *Martin Luther King, Jr.: Preacher, Freedom Fighter, Peacemaker.* Biographies. Minneapolis: Picture Window Books, 2004.

BIBLIOGRAPHY

Boyd, Herb. *We Shall Overcome.* Naperville, Ill.: Sourcebooks, 2004.

Johnson, Charles, and Bob Adelman. *King: The Photobiography of Martin Luther King, Jr.* New York: Viking Studio, 2000.

King, Martin Luther, Jr. *The Autobiography of Martin Luther King, Jr.* New York: Intellectual Properties Management in association with Warner Books, 1998.

King, Martin Luther, Jr. *A Call to Conscience: The Landmark Speeches of Dr. Martin Luther King, Jr.* New York: Intellectual Properties Management in association with Warner Books, 2001.

Stanford University. *The Papers of Martin Luther King, Jr.* The Martin Luther King Papers Project http://www.stanford.edu/group/King/index.htm.

INDEX